Classifying the Solar System Astronomy

5th Grade Astronomy & Space Science

BABY PROFESSOR
EDUCATION KIDS

Speedy Publishing LLC
40 E. Main St. #1156
Newark, DE 19711
www.speedypublishing.com
Copyright 2016

All Rights reserved. No part of this book may be reproduced or used in any way or form or by any means whether electronic or mechanical, this means that you cannot record or photocopy any material ideas or tips that are provided in this book

What objects make up our Solar System?

The Solar System is made up of the Sun (which is a star), eight planets, at least 146 moons, several asteroids and rocks, groups of comets, ice and dwarf planets. The center of the solar system is the Sun.

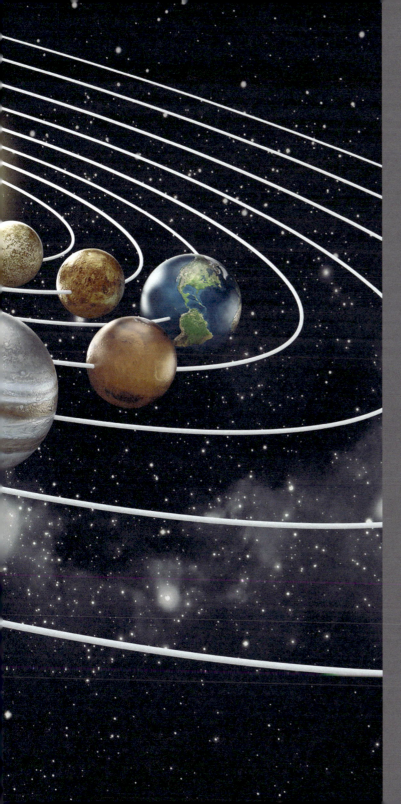

In this discussion, we will learn more about the planets in our Solar System. We will know their sizes, their distance from the Sun, how many moons each planet has, and what each planet is made of.

Jupiter, Saturn, Uranus, and Neptune are known as the giant planets, as well as the gas giants, while Mercury, Venus, Earth, and Mars are known as the small planets or the inner planets.

THE PLANETS

Mercury. It is the planet closest to the Sun. Its distance from the Sun ranges from 43 million to 66 million kilometers because it orbits the Sun in an ellipse. It's like an oval path. A Mercurial year is 88 days and a Mercurial day is equivalent to 59 Earth days.

Mercury is also known as a "lesser planet" because of its small size and is the smallest planet in our solar system. It is mostly made up of iron and a thin layer of rock with many craters. These craters were caused by asteroids that hit the planet.

The temperature of Mercury is either extremely hot or extremely cold.

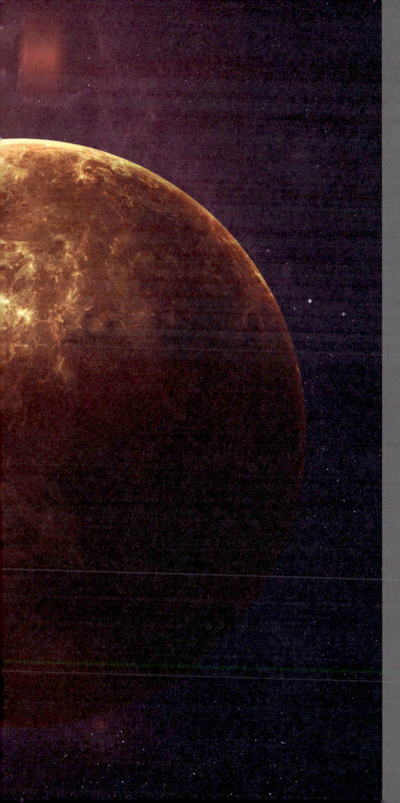

Venus. It is the second planet from the Sun and Earth's closest neighbor. The distance of Venus from the Sun averages 105 million kilometers. Its orbit around the Sun is nearly circular. A Venusian year is 225 days and a day on Venus is 243 Earth days.

Venus is considered the hottest planet in the solar system. Its hotness can even melt lead. It has almost the same size as Earth with 12100 kilometers in diameter.

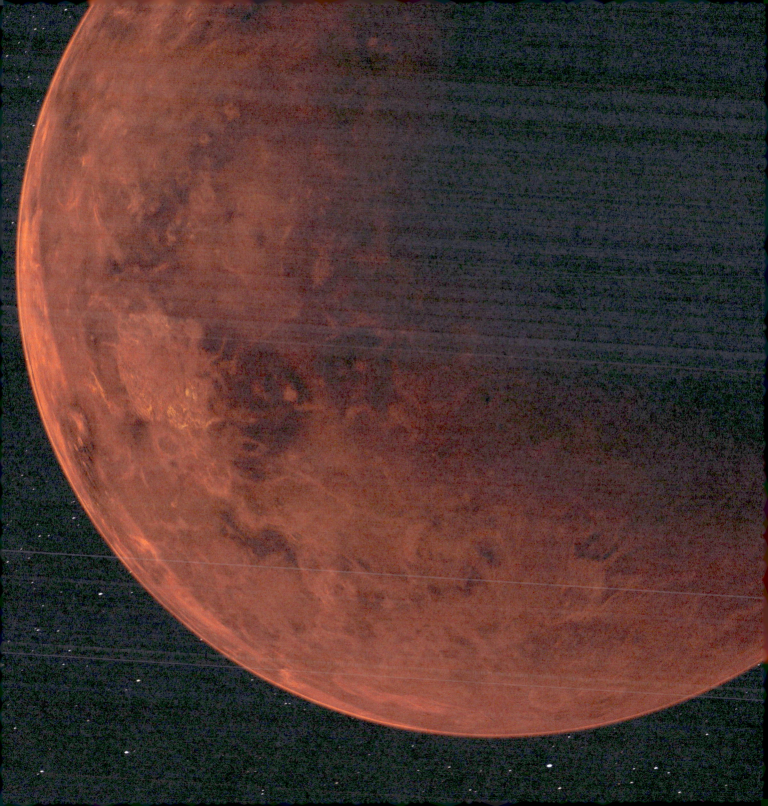

This planet can be seen many times each year with our eyes without using a telescope. Venus is covered by rocks and lava because of its many volcanoes. It has a cloudy, toxic atmosphere.

Earth. It is between the planets Venus and Mars and the third planet from the Sun. The Earth's distance from the Sun averages 150 million kilometers.

It revolves around the Sun once every 365.25 days. One year on Earth is 365 days but on its fourth year, it becomes 366 days which is what we called leap year. It has one moon. Earth rotates from west to east.

Its size has about 39000 kilometers around the equator and a diameter of about 12800 kilometers. The Earth's center is made up mostly of iron which creates a magnetic field.

The Earth's weather is either very cold or very warm. If compared to other planets, Earth's temperature is mild. It is the only planet with oceans, animals, and plants.

Mars. As the fourth planet from the Sun, Mars has an average distance of about 228 million kilometers. It orbits around the Sun in a mild ellipse.

A Martian year is equivalent to 687 days on Earth and a Martian day is 24 hours and 37 minutes. It has two moons: Phobos and Deimos.

Mars is visible from Earth. It has a diameter of around 6800 kilometers. Mars is also known as the Red Planet because there is a lot of iron oxide in the planet's surface. But the rock layer of Mars is much thicker than what is on Earth.

Mars also has weather and seasons, and averages about -12 degrees Celsius. It gets even colder during the Martian winter, dropping to -70 degrees Celsius. It has ice caps but the ice is made of carbon dioxide. Mars has deserts, mountains, and many inactive volcanoes. Olympus Mons is the largest volcano in the solar system and is even much higher than Mount Everest.

Jupiter. It is the fifth planet from the Sun and is about 778 million kilometers away from it. A year on Jupiter is equal to around twelve Earth years and a day takes only ten hours. Jupiter has 67 known moons. Europa, Io, Calisto, and Ganymede are the largest moons of Jupiter.

Jupiter's size is like 1300 Earths. It can be seen without a telescope and its brightness is next to the Moon and Venus.

The planet is made up of gas like hydrogen and helium. It has weather like Earth and other planets. The clouds keep on moving around the planet with the wind and create storms. The Great Red Spot is the most famous of all these storms.

Saturn. This planet is far from the Sun with a distance of 1427 million kilometers. As the sixth planet from the Sun, a year on Saturn takes 29.5 years. A day on Saturn is shorter than here on Earth. It has at least 53 moons.

It is the second largest planet in the solar system with a diameter of 12000 kilometers. Just like Jupiter, the planet is mostly made of hydrogen and helium and doesn't have a solid surface. Its clouds are constantly blown by winds with a speed of 1600 kilometers an hour.

Saturn has two special features which are the rings and its weight. The diameter of the rings is around 260000 kilometers and each ring is less than 15 meters thick. In total, the planet has 13 rings. It has gaps that are made from snowballs. The weight of Saturn is very light even if its size is huge.

Uranus. It is the seventh planet in the solar system and is around 3 billion kilometers away from the Sun. The orbit of the planet is an ellipse. Its size is four times the Earth's size. A year in Uranus is equivalent to 84 Earth years and a day takes a bit over seventeen hours. There are at least 15 moons around Uranus.

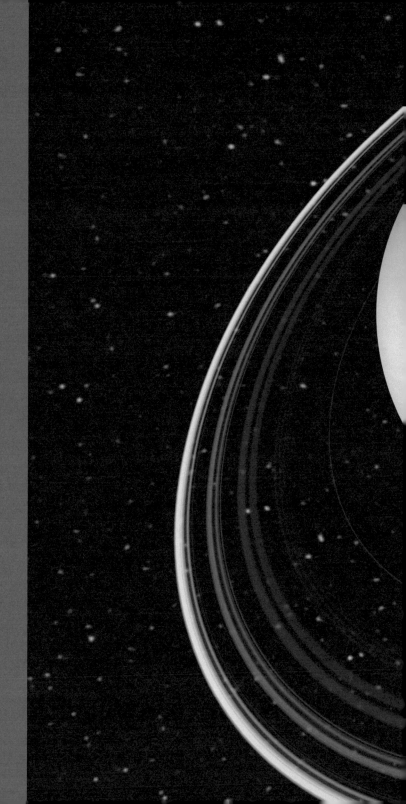

The planet can only be seen by a telescope and appears blue-green due to methane in its atmosphere. Aside from hydrogen and helium, methane is also present in the planet. It has rings, as well, but they are hard to see from telescopes on Earth or in orbit around Earth.

Uranus' South Pole faces the Sun, unlike Earth where the Equator (halfway between the poles) faces the Sun. Unlike Earth's rotation, Uranus rotates from east to west.

Neptune. The distance of Neptune from the Sun is 4.5 billion kilometers making it the eighth planet in the solar system. Its orbit is almost a perfect circle around the Sun. It takes 165 Earth years for one Uranus year and one day takes sixteen hours. The size of the planet, in diameter, is around 49500 kilometers.

Neptune's center is made up of melted rock and above it is very cold water. The color of the planet is due to methane in the atmosphere, just like Uranus. Hydrogen and helium are also abundant in Neptune. It has 14 moons.

Knowing facts about the solar system helps us realize how fortunate we are to be here on Earth. It is the only planet where life as we know it exists. Studying the classification of our system gives us a clear idea on how each planet differs from the others.

Made in United States
Troutdale, OR
12/23/2023